THE
GAME MAKER

Ian Fenn

ISBN: 0615491553
ISBN-13: 9780615491554

"Have you got even the slightest idea how long forever is? Have you ever sat for just a few hours and boggled your mind with what it means? Have you spent any time at all pondering what eternity feels like?"

CHAPTER ONE

THE GAME MAKER

My life had become rather boring of recent, especially the last fifty billion years—now they **really** dragged. That was why I made a visit to the Game Maker. I had heard that he had recently made a very special game and I was looking for something really challenging to do with the next twenty-five billion years.

If you are fully aware of your immortality then I know what you may be thinking right now: "Fifty billion years can pass in the wink of an eye; you should try spending a few trillion stuck in one darn universe"— and I would not argue with you.

The trouble with time really starts when you are crossing off each million years as they pass, as I am doing right now. It really can be like watching paint dry or, in my case, waiting for the first sign of intelligent life to appear in this Milky Way galaxy. I have been here from the very start of this galaxy and all the others. I was here before the first stars had yet to form, which I know to you might seem to be a very long time. It has, by comparison, been a mere blink of an eye since the first human appeared on the Earth. This appearance was one event for which I had been waiting patiently, and when it finally did happen, I could at last begin work on the planet Earth, part of my quest. Not that the appearance of humans hailed the arrival of anything approaching true intelligence, but to be fair to you all, that is not really possible given the rules of the game. When you understand what a human being really is (which this book will explain) then you will understand that nothing you believe in is what it seems, and I don't mean in some mystic way; I mean it really is not at all what it seems.

If you are thinking I am being rather unfair or even arrogant saying that there have been no intelligent humans then perhaps I should clarify what I mean by intelligence. The intelligence I speak of is that of an immortal being who knows exactly who and what they are, a being operating in total consciousness. This type of consciousness is only possible outside of this universe and is far beyond what is commonly known here on Earth as enlightenment. If you have spent your life striving for enlightenment, that idea may not be easy to accept but, nonetheless, it is truth.

This will all make perfect sense to you if you continue to read; trust me: after you finish this book, you will be clearer on who you are and why you are here, and you will see why absolutely nothing made any real sense without the information you are about to discover, and that includes enlightenment.

I have, over the last thousands of years, spoken to many humans about immortality and how tough and, at times, boring it can be. You can imagine that they often think I am ungrateful and that the gift is wasted on me. They then become certain that I must be some kind of fool when I tell them that the reason I came to this universe was to spend a few billion years simply for my own amusement and that it really does not have some special meaning or reason for existing at all. I understand this reaction, as it seems rather irreverent and dismissive of the miracle of creation or somehow devaluing their life's purpose. When you have so little time as you humans do then you cannot be blamed for overvaluing its place in the grand scheme of things. However, it is my hope that, after reading this book, you will understand more about what it means to be immortal and you will also see why the Game Maker is one of the most popular immortal beings ever to create himself. You will also see why a visit to sample his skills is an inevitable event at some point in eternity.

You have, as a human, only about seventy to eighty years of life to endure, and yet I often hear thoughts about how bored you can get; well, my friends, try living for a billion-trillion years, just for starters, and then talk to me about boredom. Seriously, have you got even the slightest idea how long forever is? Have you ever sat for just a few hours and boggled your mind with what it means? Have you spent any time at all pondering what eternity feels like?

Okay, it is probably a daft question to ask a being who is stuck in a body with a tiny lifespan; maybe I can help with some clarifying imagery. Imagine, if you will, a very hard piece of granite rock, just like the sort you make your kitchen countertops from, and now imagine one of these the size of a galaxy. Then imagine the length of time that the water from one dripping faucet would take to wear this galactic rock down to nothing. This universe will almost certainly be over before that could occur.

Got that length of time fixed in your head? I'm guessing you will be struggling to get your mind around it, as it is more than most can comprehend, but please keep going. Now, let us multiply that mind-boggling time by a billion or so and you are not even slightly close to what eternity feels like.

The alternative to being aware of these massive lengths of time is the sleeping state of oneness that some earthly philosophers and mystics have imagined or glimpsed briefly and then attempted to explain as a place where there is no time, or that perhaps all of time exists in a single moment of now. This is not entirely true; it is more of a place where there is nothing at all, no story to follow, and no consequences (consecutive sequences), but it is nevertheless a handy place to go for a break from the constant movement of a universe of time. It can be relaxing for a while but the lack of stable, solid creations to play and interact with is only appealing for a while. Like I said, it's nice for a break.

Thinking of this makes me want to take a relaxing, long snooze. Would you excuse me for a moment? Aaahh!

zzzzzzzzz............

..................ZZZZZZZ

"Once you understand your true nature, you will see that there are no goals that are better or more right or more just or more worthy than any other, and that you may as well enjoy your life to the full."

CHAPTER TWO

THE GAME.

Okay, I'm back. I popped off for a small break there—in fact, about one hundred thousand years of your time passed since I wrote the words above, which, incidentally, I have had to completely rewrite. They were originally written in some extremely ancient (by your standards) text from another planet, a planet that I am embarrassed to say I seem to have lost. It was parked around a particular star when I last saw it; it's not the first planet I have lost and probably won't be the last. When you are immortal, these things happen more than you might think. It's not that I am careless; it is simply because there is no hurry in finishing anything except the urgency that we place upon ourselves and, to be honest, since I came to this universe, I have been a little forgetful. Hopefully I can apply myself and finish this book and not have to rewrite it and finish it on yet another planet. This book did not start out speaking about humans, but it works just as well here on Earth, and unless I told you it was a rewrite, I am sure you would never have guessed. There are a few other books on sale here on Earth that are rewrites from other planets, but I am not at liberty to tell you which they are for universal copyright reasons.

So where was I? Ah, yes, the Game Maker and immortality.

In order to understand why an immortal being would want to use the services of a game maker, there are some ideas on games that need to be discussed.

There are two key elements to consider when looking at any game: they are, first of all, a task to do and, second, a limited amount of time to do it in. Right now, for example, you have a challenge in front of you. It is this book; it has a certain number of words and you have decided to begin reading it with, I hope, the intention to finish it, yes?

You know that you have a finite amount of time in which to finish the book, i.e., you will have to read it before you die. So we can see that there is a certain thing to accomplish and you only have a set period in which to accomplish it. Would you agree that this is true of everything you do in life? Pretty much that way, isn't it? That is why, from an immortal point of view, it really is fun to be you. I mean a human, not you in particular.

Being human means you have very little time to achieve a whole list of oh-so-important things, and while some of you set your sights pretty low, others aim for lofty, almost out-of-reach heights. In this book, I am going to tell you some really good news: there are some hidden truths about this universe that mean you can all be more relaxed and have more fun. Let's face it: you could all do with more fun.

The truth is that, even though in any single lifetime you can never find all of the answers to life's mysteries no matter how hard you search, many of you will still spend your whole life searching and feeling you are missing something.

There may also be a constant haunting feeling that there is a secret that you are just not getting, a secret that others may know but are not sharing. Don't worry; this feeling is perfectly normal for a human, and because of the rules of the game, it is impossible to completely get rid of it, even if you became a member of every elite or secret power group or hidden holy order.

I hope through reading this book that you experience more relaxation, and that it can help you have more fun with your life. The fact that you found this book shows that you are one who is seeking, and that you have a built-in knowingness that there is something hidden going on in this universe, and you want to find out what it is. From your various efforts, you might have already worked out that the answers are not going to come from breathing exercises, no matter how advanced, nor from more meditation. Such practices and others like them are really great ways to use up some time and quiet the mind, but will not change one thing about the rules of what is really going on here. They will not show you the truth.

Some of you have this knowledge that there is a hidden truth in greater amounts than others, and I will explain why this is so as we go along.

It will all become much clearer as I explain about the game of this universe that I and other immortals have been playing for billions of years, and that it actually directly involves you…and, yes, I do mean YOU.

My intention is to help you see the reality of this universe and your part in it because I know that if you can grasp what is really going on, you will all be instantly more relaxed, and you will see there is nothing that will give you the great happiness you seek—not in one human life, in any case.

The small games you can play as a human of building business empires and owning bright red, shiny, fast cars, your own jet, and all the gold you can eat are not bad reasons for living, as some people with more "green ideas" might wish to tell you. Once you understand your true nature, you will see that there are no goals that are better or more right or more just or more worthy than any other, and that you may as well enjoy your life to the full. The problem, of course, is that you have such a small lifespan in which to do any of it, so that if you want that Ferrari and don't yet have it, you had better get on with it fast. If you are a seeker of enlightenment and the ultimate truth, then you obviously still feel there is more to know, and regardless of your age, there really is very little time left to find the answer to the ultimate questions, so you had better get back to those breathing techniques and chanting sacred mantras before it's too late and you run out of breath completely.

That brings us back nicely to the subject of having something to achieve and a set time to achieve it. These two elements form the basic rules that apply to every game ever played, either on a board or, more broadly speaking, in your life. From the larger goals like buying the house of your dreams to the smaller, simpler goals like having dinner, they all share one common factor: they are all on the clock, from the beginning to the end.

By contrast, when you are an immortal, all-powerful being, there is no reason at all to get something done in a hurry; time is something you have plenty of. Just to be clear here about time for those who are seeking enlightenment: yes, I know there are places or planes of existence where time does not exist at all; I have spent a lot of <u>no time</u> in them, and, frankly you are welcome to them. You will understand this comment more as you read on, but just ask yourself this: if it's so good, why are you here?

Can you imagine a game without a time limit of some sort? A chess game that went on for ten thousand years? Played by generation after generation of family members, with only one move every ten years? Not likely to happen with the human lifespan or attention span, is it? What would you say, then, if I told you that I have been playing a game that has lasted billions of years, just for the fun of it? Well, that's exactly what I have been doing, and it is what this book is going to explore, but first let us look at more usual games played by humans.

Most of the best games we play require a mystery; they require a puzzle or a skill to be learned. Take the classic board game of Clue, for example, in which we have to find out who killed whom, with what weapon, and in which room of the house. The point of the game is to solve a mystery faster than the other players. Again, it is a task to do with a time constraint, just like most of your life. If we took away the need to find the answer before the other players, if we took the time element out of the game, it would lose all the fun, would it not?

The trouble with games when you are an immortal, all-powerful being is that there can be no mystery. So what possible game would hold the interest of a being who can be in every point of the universe and in every time all at once? How could you hide the answers from them so that they could have the pleasure inherent in discovering a secret? In the game of Clue, for example, they could simply look with x-ray vision into the envelope containing the "who done it" cards and tell us all the answers before the game ever started, or look forward or backward in time to see the cards being placed into or withdrawn from the envelope. This would, of course, render the game useless. With super powers, mystery games seem as pointless as playing hide and seek in a warehouse with white walls and white floors and all players dressed in bright orange with nothing to hide behind. One, two, three…here I come. Oh, there you all are! Shall we play again?

Like wise, the game of attempting to gain enough wealth to the point where you can declare that you are finally happy would hold no challenge, either. A being such as I could simply manifest from thin air any of the things money can buy or simply create a mountain-sized heap of dollars immediately when the game started. The board game Monopoly would be no fun if you started it with a million dollars each. You could all buy every street you landed on and then immediately place hotels on each one. The game would then take forever as you simply collected rent from each other as you landed on each player's property. This would be a pointless game because there would be zero difficulty or skill and certainly no feeling of satisfaction. You see, enjoying achievements requires that they be difficult. Just as games for adult humans are more complex than children's games, so it is that games played by immortals are even harder.

The other problem with being immortal and playing games is that time has no meaning.

When you know you can't die and nothing can harm you, then it kind of takes away the urgency to get anything done. If the point of a game is to achieve a certain goal but there is no time limit, then you have no measure as to how well you are doing, no sense of urgency, and no sense of satisfaction. You would not care about how soon you finish because time it is not a part of the game. You, as a human, however, have a time limit built in automatically from birth; you have a few rules that make the game of being human urgent and focused. One of the most important is called death. Death is a killer of a reason to get on with things, and it brings with it a sense of urgency. Add to this urgency a built-in feeling of not ever being satisfied but not knowing why, and you have the recipe for a planet full of very busy little beings.

Death is the main reason you are all scampering around in ever-faster methods of transport, using ever-faster ways to send each other ever-increasing amounts of information. Death is driving all this big hurry; in fact, without it, you may not have invented the motor-car or the mobile phone for a very long time to come.

You really do owe all the modern time-saving ways of life to your impending deaths. You owe your drive to get things done today to the fact that you will be dying very soon. Death, for a human being, makes everything more urgent, and as we have already discussed, it is the set time we have to do something in that is one of the required elements of any good game.

Time is one of the most important aspects of a human life or a short game, and in your case, that is pretty much the same thing. In order for an immortal being like me to enjoy a game, I, too, have to respect the aspect of time. A limited lifespan in human form is one rule even we do not break.

That leads us nicely to the other main rules of any game.

Rules are a set of agreements that all players have to abide by in order for the game to have structure, for it to have a set beginning and an ultimate goal or end. Rules also make it possible for the game to be a common experience that can be shared by all who play it.

Rules are what make the game; they define its difference and its mode of play. They define how it differs from other games and they give the player instructions as to what he can and cannot do; for example, you cannot start with ten million dollars in Monopoly. If you have played Monopoly, then you know it would render the game boring if you could have all the money you want right at the start.

So it is in your life also. If you strive for some goal then the striving is part of the reward of finally getting what you seek, and, in most cases, in fact, the striving turns out to be the best part. After achieving a goal, often you will just go right on with setting new, even higher goals. You know this is true; you want the highest high you can get: the best score, the bigger house, the newer car, the best meal you can make, and on and on. Many of you even push for greater and greater awareness or what some call "enlightenment." It does not matter what it is; as humans and as immortals, we all share this sense of wanting to have more, get more, be more, create more. It is the growth that is built into our basic essence.

So these rules help us play a meaningful game; they help us to define things like how long have we got, what the goal or purpose is, and what we need in order to play the game.

Team games require that each player has a role and must stick to the individual rules for that role. For example, if he is a goalkeeper in the game of soccer, he can use his hands, unlike his team members, who can never use their hands on the field except to throw the ball from the side lines. We have agreed roles to play and we have items to play them with, such as balls, goal posts, playing cards, chess pieces, boards to play on, etc. We have a certain arena within which to play; we have a set place within which the rules are applied. When we switch between games, we can change the rules, such as when playing volleyball, where all the players can use their hands.

So I think we all agree that a game has to have rules, goals, and a time limit to be an interesting game, yes?

Rules can also be agreed limits to our normal powers; for example, sports are all full of rules that limit the force we are capable of using. In the game of American football or rugby, we have players using great force to take down their opponents; however, they stop very short of deliberately smashing limbs and breaking heads, even though this would more permanently solve the problem of a charging opposition. Instead, what we do in these games is agree to hold back, to use our strength in a limited way.

We do not use all our powers.

Look at it in another way, if you will: in a game of marbles, for example, where we try to win all the opponent's marbles, or a game of cards, such as poker, played for money, it would be easier to just beat the opposition over the head and take all the money rather than take the time to beat them with skill. In other words, the end result is not at all the point of the game; it is the fact that we have to get the result through skill and cunning rather than sheer force. If we did not limit our use of power in certain ways, there could be no games at all. Every human has to limit the force they use and play by rules or there would be very few of you left alive except for a few of the strongest, most ruthless killers holding all the land and toys, and no one left to play with.

I think we can agree, therefore, that in order to play certain games, we have to also agree to limits on our powers, or there is no game.

So how, then, can the Game Maker that I mentioned on page one of this book have invented a game for myself and fellow immortals to play that is a highly complicated puzzle, a giant of a game with many hard mysteries to be solved? Remember that, as a super powerful immortal being, I can see everything, I know everything, and nothing can be hidden from me.

How can it be that an immortal with absolutely no limitations plays a game of mystery like this? How can I be puzzled by a puzzle, however complex? How can anything be hidden from me?

The answer to this question affects you so profoundly that I must, at this point, warn you that it could be shocking and could change the way you live the rest of this life. I must ask that if you continue to read this book, you agree to read the <u>whole</u> book. If you don't read the whole book, you may miss some vital information that may lead you to experience the opposite effect than the one it was meant to help you have—the effect of freeing you from illusion and helping you have a more relaxed and joy-filled life.

What you are about to find out could change everything you ever thought about everything you ever thought.

But please relax; with the right attitude and a spirit of fun, it will only increase the sense of adventure that you really should be living life from. After all, the entire universe really is just a giant game. And you are here to play it.

"The universe, as you call it, is in fact the arena within which the grand game of the Game Maker can be played, and it is a sealed-off, separated place within which certain rules and laws can be made to work."

CHAPTER THREE

LET THE GAMES BEGIN.

I had heard it was an amazing game. Every being who played it so far was full of praise for it and many could not wait to play again, but none would tell me anything specific because one of the rules of the game was that you could not discuss it with others. The point of the secrecy was obvious as the entire point of the game lay in its difficulty and its mystery.

The game was originally played by groups of hundreds of thousands, and, more recently, hundreds of millions of beings at the same time, and another game was due to start in a few million years so I had to make my decision to join this particular game without delay or the places might all be gone. I understand that it has recently become such a popular game that there are now hundreds of universes running at any one time to accommodate the demand.

The game always starts in the same way with what your scientists have called the big bang, and ends when all those who are playing have solved the puzzles and worked out how to leave, at which point there will then be a big collapse, if we use the same analogy. Neither of which, incidentally, would really be accurate. If you imagine the action of blowing up a balloon you would be closer in image to what happens at the start of a universe than a large explosion, and at the end, if you let all the pressure out of the balloon, then the way it collapses would better describe the end of each universe.

You need to understand what exists outside of your universe and the causation method of making a universe to be able to understand this. If you are missing ninety-nine pieces of a hundred-piece jigsaw puzzle, you can imagine and create stories about what the whole picture might look like based on the tiny piece you posses, and although the theoretical complete picture you may make could seem to be plausible, chances are it would be a million miles from the truth. If I gave you one piece of a jigsaw of a city view from another civilized planet, and the piece I gave you was a solid blue piece of the sky, would you have the slightest chance of knowing anything about the truth of the whole jigsaw image? Could you take that piece of blue sky and make the slightest assumptions about the appearance of the alien city?

You currently exist inside a closed system, rather like a balloon, and because of that everything you can ever measure or know is that which can be measured or known within the closed system. This is why your science has theories like the big bang, but without the slightest, tiniest clue about what caused it all to happen in the first place. To understand the causation of the universe requires knowledge of what lies outside the closed bubble of the visible universe. In fact, the entire point of this universe is that it is a closed bubble.

There is no way to see outside of it with any understanding because all of the science you might try to use to understand where it came from is built upon laws and rules and theories made from inside the closed system—even quantum physics, which your science community is so proud of, is still applying rules, imagined or real, from within a closed system.

The universe, as you call it, is in fact the arena within which the grand game of the Game Maker can be played, and it is a sealed-off, separated place within which certain rules and laws can be made to work.

It is required to be sealed by distinct borders, within which certain rules apply, for the same reason we have a sports arena or defined area such as a chess board. It has to have defined borders to fulfill its reason for being made.

The chess board serves as a fine example of rules and laws and closed systems.

Take a chess piece like the knight; it is defined not as much by the fact that it looks like a horse than the fact that it moves in a very set way. It can move two squares in one direction and then one square to the left or right or up or down, depending on its position on the board. All other chess pieces have similar set rules about the moves they can make. They must make these moves one square at a time, or several, depending on what rules apply to the type of piece they are. The squares of the board are two colors, normally black and white, and are of a certain size. There are a fixed number of squares on the board and the board itself is a larger square made of these smaller squares.

This is a space within which certain laws and rules apply: it has certain math in place; it has a set design. The chess board is a fixed system and no matter who plays it, if they follow the rules, the eventual outcome is the same. The game can vary, the players can make their own moves, but in the end, the outcome is always the same: one player wins or a stalemate is declared; there can be no other outcomes. In a system of fixed rules and laws and math, such as chess, we can also make up some theories to explain the game. We can make a computer that can play the game better than most humans because it is simply a game of set rules and moves. The computer looks at all the possible moves and makes a choice. As clever as it might appear to be, it is still only working with the choices that it is allowed to make within the rules of a closed system.

The thing is, if we took that computer program using the closed system rules of chess and applied it to the closed-system rules of the board game Monopoly, it would make no sense at all; it would certainly be no use whatsoever in helping you win.

So it is with the closed system of your universe; your rules and your math work here, but they make not a jot of sense outside of it.

This is why your scientists will never, ever truly understand the big bang; they are using the rules and laws from within a closed system (the universe), which was created using the laws and math of a place outside of these rules. The theory that explains it all, as some are now seeking, will never come, and if someone finally declares they have a theory to explain it all and it does not start out by telling you the universe was created just to play a game in, then I can assure you what follows will be pure guess work and will be missing all the actual math and facts they need to really tell you anything.

"In this compressed universe, saying it's just an illusion as a speeding car hits you at a hundred miles an hour will most certainly be the last daft comment you make. You might want to try it in a less dense universe for a much better result, where the comment would also actually be more real."

CHAPTER FOUR

A QUICK SCIENCE LESSON.

I was not going to get into the science of this universe, but after considering how much speculation there is on the subject, I thought it best to point your scientists in the right direction and save them from a lot of wasted time. It may not save them time in the near future, but at some point in the future it will.

This universe was created when energy was, in effect, blown into a large balloon and compressed (it is the best visual way to explain it). Energy made to behave in a certain way forms what we call "matter," and compressed matter is what this universe is made from. This entire universe is compressed, it is dense, and it is solidly and rigidly three-dimensional. There are, by comparison, places that are three-dimensional in appearance but with less compression, and therefore they have less rigid rules. In these other places, there may still be walls and seemingly solid objects, but they are walls that it is possible to walk through; this can only occur in less compressed universes. This particular universe is, however, for all intents and purposes, as solid as they get.

I get quite a laugh out of quantum physics as discussed in bars and meditation centers alike, where people can be heard saying, "You know, everything is just energy and it's all an illusion." While this is true in a sense, it is a pointless and somewhat misleading thing to say. In this compressed universe, saying it's just an illusion as a speeding car hits you at a hundred miles an hour will most certainly be the last daft comment you make. You might want to try it in a less dense universe for a much better result, where the comment would also actually be more real.

It's funny because in less dense universes, where a car could just pass right through you with no harm and everything is an illusion created by thoughts affecting the energy matrix around you, no one hangs about in bars or meditation centers making such comments, and there is no need for a car, in any case.

Back to the science.... Matter, when compressed, changes, just as the gas blown into a balloon changes in density. If compressed enough, gas will turn into a liquid but it will only stay in this changed form as long as it remains compressed. You have seen how the liquid gas of a cigarette lighter turns back into a gas when it escapes through the opened value; in fact, it really wants to go back to its uncompressed state and will escape as fast as it can.

We can agree, then, that matter alters when compressed. In this dense universe, you can have no idea how matter behaves more fluidly and easily when in its more natural, relaxed state. This is because even in the so-called vacuum of space, it is still compressed. Space itself is pressurized; it only appears as a vacuum in comparison to the higher pressures that exist in the atmosphere and in the depths of the seas here on Earth and other planets.

The problem of making measurements of the pressure of this universe is in your scientific instruments; the very instruments you make here are themselves made from pressurized matter in a space that is pressurized. Instruments to measure things are subject to limitations. If you take a device that measures how full a tank of fuel is in a car and try to use that same device to measure how much fuel is in a similar tank in the weightlessness of space, it would not be any good at all. The reason is that it uses a float that goes up and down with the fuel level, and in space the fuel would float around in the tank and form into spheres, rendering your fuel gauge useless. You could measure the weight of a person using bathroom scales while scuba diving at fifty feet down in the sea, but the diver has buoyancy and so will appear much lighter than he does on dry land. Change the environment, and the same measuring device gives a whole new reading.

So I think you can see that unless you know a less dense universe exists, you will not know just how compressed this one is because you just do not have a way to measure it, and as you are not even aware of it in the first place, you would not know to look for the evidence.

This simple but important missing piece of data (that this is a compressed universe) leads to all kinds of misinterpretations. The balloon is a good example in many ways—for instance, if we put a tiny hole in its skin, the compressed air inside cannot wait to escape and rushes out of the hole; the bigger the hole, the faster it escapes. In fact, at the point of escape, the air momentarily becomes even more compressed as the molecules of air rush into the same space to escape; there is a turbulent swirling inside the balloon just above the hole. This swirling motion is similar to that of water as it swirls around an open drain hole in a bath. Black holes are, in fact, simply holes in the universe through which compressed matter is escaping back to its less dense and more natural state. The black hole may appear to grow only because it is, in effect, an expanding hole. It does not grow, as some believe, because it is accumulating more and more matter. It is a region of increased compression but this is more like a shock wave caused by the rush of compressed space and planets and stars being blown and pushed by the matter behind them that is also desperate to get out. To visualize this more easily, imagine a hundred-foot-high tube about three feet across and filled with water. There is a pipe at the base of the tube with a valve. The water at the bottom is under pressure because of the water pushing down on it from above, and so as we open the valve at the bottom and the water starts to gush out, it is, in fact, the water at the top of the one-hundred-foot tube that is pushing out the water at the bottom.

The matter rushing to the black hole is being pushed hard by all the compressed matter behind it... the rest of the universe is pushing toward the hole. The reason galaxies swirl the way they do is because they are swirling down a giant drain hole: the black hole scientists have discovered recently at the center of most galaxies.

There was a time before the holes began to appear when there were no galaxies, when stars and matter were spread more evenly through space. Eventually all stars and planets will disappear as each galaxy ends in a final hiss. The universe will shrink and collapse like a deflating balloon, and that will be that—at least until the board is reset for another game.

Now, of course, scientists don't believe that this is a closed-system, compressed universe and so they cannot imagine that matter can escape to somewhere outside— hence, the idea of a super dense ball of crushed matter that they think is a black hole. They have had to invent a whole new set of theories to explain how an entire galaxy can finally fit into something the size of a football when the black hole has eaten the galaxy. When they figure out it is really a hole through which all the stuff of the galaxy has gone, into another, less dense universe, their headaches will stop and they will all be able to spend more time having fun. Of course, they are simply doing what they are made for, which is searching for keys.

This explanation leads to more questions: what is going on in the less compressed universe? The answer is much the same as here, but less solid. Reality outside this dense universe is not simply one area; there are many regions with many rules and physics involved. You may have traveled to these regions when your dense body is asleep; ever been in a dream where you can fly? This is often when you have traveled to a region where reality is less dense and the rules are different.

In this book, I will explain the game and its rules. As I have said, the board of the game is your universe, and to you that might seem implausible simply because it is such an enormous creation just for a game, but remember that this is a game made by an all-powerful being for similar beings to play, and it has to be very complex and take a long time or it would not keep us amused for long. Our games are not played in hours; they are played in eternity, not unlike the British game of cricket, which, although not played over an eternity, can easily seem that way.

That's the end of the science lesson: you live in a compressed universe. Get over it.

The thing is, in order to join in this incredible game and for it to be enjoyable, we have to become limited and agree to stay limited for the entire length of the game.

These agreed limitations then set the scene for a tough-to-solve mystery, which is the entire point of this game, and, as it turns out, the entire reason for your small lifespan as a human.

CHAPTER FIVE

MORE ON THE RULES.

If your toy companies were to advertise this game, the ad might go something like this:

The Universe, a Game by the Master Game Maker
Enter a magical maze, spread across infinite distances, and solve the hardest puzzle of all time. Search in endless worlds of matter and energy separated by vast tracts of space.

Be the first to uncover all the mysteries and gather all the keys—the hidden keys that will then allow you to escape this most difficult of mazes, the most difficult yet to be created.

How long will it take you? Will you beat the fastest time? Will you be the champion of the universe? The ultimate game starts soon and finishes in approximately thirty billion years (or when all have found their way out, whichever is sooner).

Disclaimer: Please note the Game Maker and his helpers will not be held responsible for any being who is lost inside the game for what might be considered an inconveniently long length of time. There are no guarantees that the game will not take much longer to solve than the advertised times. If you have plans for next ten billion years (the fastest it has been completed so far), please notify the Game Maker and his staff before entering so that you can have an early wake-up call scheduled; should you not have escaped the game in time to meet your plans and you did not arrange a wake-up call, we cannot be held responsible for missed appointments in eternity. For your pleasure, it is recommended that you allow a minimum of fifteen billion years in order to enjoy the game without interruption. Furthermore, we will not be held responsible for pain or suffering, which can be the result of forgetting who you are. Forgetting who you are is a required component of the game. The rules of the game are available to view on request.

As I explained earlier, in order for there to be a game, there has to be a goal and a set time in which to achieve it. The best games, just as the best films, have a mystery that is to be solved before the film or game is over. A game for a super being needs to be a big game, preferably one with a really big mystery that is not at all easy to solve. However, one of the things we know about omnipotent beings is that mysteries are really hard to keep from them, as they tend to be everywhere at the same time.

This is where the Game Maker earns his reputation as a master. In the game of the universe, the first thing we do when we begin playing is go through a memory-inhibiting energy field that, in effect, creates a separated being; that area of our being that has memory or continuity is put into a holding area, and at the same time our creative powers are reduced somewhat, all of which happens outside this universe, and so that is really as much as one can say about it. The way it is achieved is way beyond the boundaries of any reality you can ever dream up; you simply have no frame of reference to understand it. If you imagine trying to explain quantum physics to a moth, that would be quite similar. It would probably say, "Oh, look at the pretty light…I must fly toward it," as it headed off to the nearest lightbulb and called out over its shoulder, "Sorry, what was that about a particle also being a wave?"

The thing is, in order to join in this incredible game and for it to be enjoyable, we have to become limited and agree to stay limited for the entire length of the game.

These agreed limitations then set the scene for a tough-to-solve mystery, which is the entire point of this game, and, as it turns out, the entire reason for your small lifespan as a human.

The game of the universe is played across the vast board that you see when you look out of your window, the one you see when you gaze into space, and the one your Hubble space telescope has managed to look a little more deeply into in recent years.

The game is being played across the entire width and depth of this vast space. It is a game played on countless planets in billions of galaxies. There can be millions or billions of beings just like me playing the game at any one time, and all of them start the game at the same time. This start is usually the moment your science is now calling the big bang, and it ends for each player only when they collect all the keys needed by solving the mysteries of the game. When a player finds enough keys, this allows them to finally escape the game and regain their lost memory and powers, the same memory that was checked at the door to the universe, rather like you would hand your coat to the doorman when entering a night club.

It is a good thing that you don't need to retain a ticket in order to get back your memory and your full powers since you would most certainly have lost it during the fifteen to thirty billion years you can spend in the game. Instead of a numbered ticket handed to a doorman, you have to present the correct number of keys to the gatekeeper. The keys which are in the main experiences rather than physical keys, have been incredibly hard to locate and even harder to correctly experience.

So how is the game of the universe played? There are several aims of the game, the ultimate being to beat every other player. The main goal of this game, then, is not enlightenment, as you already had that and agreed to give it up in order to play. The point is also not to grow spiritually, as you are already an omnipotent being, and neither is it to discover your immortality, as that is your birthright. No, in fact, the biggest goal of this particular existence is to escape it as fast as you can. It is to find your way out of the universe, and this can only be done when you have collected enough of the keys that have been hidden around what is really the most gigantic board game. I hate breaking this news to people who are seekers, as many think there is some hidden purpose or some process involved where they eventually, through study or by letting go, can become the enlightened being, but, in fairness, they don't usually listen to me since they mostly think I am missing some very important secret. They may look down their spiritual noses and believe that I obviously "don't get it," that I lost my mind, and that only they really "get it."

Spiritual arrogance is very common in humans and serves as a way to stop all the seeking and of finally having an answer to the mystery that feels comfortable and workable. It brings some certainty to the uncertainty, it appears to solve a mystery, and it can appear to bring greater peace. The expanded awareness that some practices seek to bring is, in fact, becoming more aware of the being that is operating in them rather than a greater version of human consciousness. In others words, the puppet becomes aware of the strings and, through the strings, senses something greater, and feels in touch with the life-force and intelligence that is operating them. I hope that does not seem harsh; it is not the best way to describe the situation, which I shall cover in more depth shortly. Think of the strings for now as the conduit through which the intuition and nudges you often feel can flow.

As I said, first and foremost, the goal is to escape the game. A further goal is to be the overall winner. This is achieved by collecting the required number of keys to escape the universe with the least number of lives used, including human lives. The next goal involves speed, and it is to collect the keys needed to escape the universe in the least amount of time.

The overall winner in each game is the one who solves the puzzle with the least use of incarnations or bodies and in the shortest amount of time.

If we did not have this competitive edge to the game then one could simply make a billion intelligent life forms and run them all at once on every possible key-bearing planet or region of activity. By regions, I mean those that people may refer to as the astral planes (those less dense physical regions that surround the Earth and other planets). Actually, because we have limitations in this universe, we cannot run more than a few hundred bodies at the same time. It dilutes our attention and, after a certain point, becomes a point-less thing to do as we make beings that are less and less capable.

Those are the main rules, then: to collect all the keys we need as quickly as possible and with the least lives needed.

"So to recap, a human is a flesh body filled with varying degrees of projected awareness from a voluntarily limited immortal being who is playing a game but has forgotten that it is a game and that he actually agreed to play it in the first place. Simple really, isn't it?"

CHAPTER SIX

THE PIECES OF THE GAME, OR WHAT IS A HUMAN BEING?

So this is where the shock may begin for your average enlightenment seeker, if he or she allows him- or herself to believe what I am about to explain. I do not know how to put this in an easier way, so I will give it to you straight.

As a human, you cannot become an immortal being and you cannot achieve enlightenment; this is because you are, in fact, simply a projected field of energy of an immortal being like me. You are just one of hundreds or thousands of creations made to explore the universe by a being that needs to make a physical body mixed with the spiritual essence of himself (or herself, if I must be politically correct, which, in the interest of harmony, let's pretend I am) in order to explore this universe of compressed matter. In other words, in order to explore here, you need to own and operate at least one compressed-matter body.

We create these bodies and then project our awareness into them. This awareness you call consciousness will, upon the death of the body, simply withdraw back into the being that was projecting it. It is a little more complex than that because the being that is doing the projecting and withdrawing is also a limited version of itself (it can't remember who it is fully and has lost much of its powers) in order to play the game of the universe.

So to recap, a human is a flesh body filled with varying degrees of projected awareness from a voluntarily limited immortal being who is playing a game but has forgotten that it is a game and that he actually agreed to play it in the first place. Simple really, isn't it?

Now, if you stay with me on this, there is no need for despair or upset at all, because this simply clarifies a few things that you might not have thought through fully before, and I hope that you will soon be able to see why all of this is actually a really good thing. It does not mean that you really don't exist or have no constant existence after death.

You might ask, "What about my own memories? What about my past lives?"

To better understand all of what I am telling you, it will help to look at the past life idea. People have past life recall, or at least some do, and others may have experienced leaving their bodies in some way, and so they tend to think of themselves as having survived death somehow...hmmm, but that is not really so. In fact, when we make a human form, there are also made, at the same time, various lower-density versions, what some call the astral body, etc. So the being simply continues on with the next body that is still functioning. These bodies will not disappear until we, as the super beings or higher self, leave the dense universe altogether. The fact that you continue to be aware after death and have also at times had glimpses or contact with others created by your higher self is what creates the confusion. You see, the author of this book, my creation, Ian Fenn, has a definite personality and mannerisms, and has developed all kinds of emotional responses and feelings, etc., and all of that does not die but continues in the remaining, less dense versions of himself. What happens when the game really is over is that all that he is and was will be absorbed back into me, the one projecting the power, the juice that ran all that mind stuff and those layers of bodies. The memories of that life will be stored in me forever.

Ian Fenn has, during his dreams and meditation, connected to another one of my creations as a German man in the last war, and he did at one time believe it was one of his past lives; he also believed he had a past life as a Lakota Indian in the Black Hills of South Dakota in the USA. However, he now understands that these are all really just my creations having awareness of each other.

They are not Ian Fenn's past lives; they are my other creations. Can you see the difference? So can the being experiencing itself as Ian Fenn become me? Can he become an immortal being? Can the part become the whole? Can one memory about one minute of one hour of your life be thought to be your entire history? Can Ian Fenn become the enlightened immortal being? No, he cannot because the immortal essence that allows him to be aware and empowers his mind energy to think thoughts and create its own personality is mine.

I am his true awareness, and I am already enlightened because I am an immortal being. If an actor played the part of an actor who was playing a part, ask yourself, "Could the character the actor plays become enlightened?"

This is simply saying that all that enlightenment is, in the way it is commonly used, is knowing that your essence is greater and more powerful than the evidence of what you appear to be, that you feel this but cannot quite put your finger on it. That you may connect with other creations of your higher self; you may also experience the consciousness you have been given floating outside the body in some way. That you mistake this as meaning that you in your current form with your current thoughts and feelings are the true being, that somehow you as John, Jo, Pete, Lisa, Sharon, etc., are, in fact, the immortal soul. But really your consciousness as a person is borrowed. It's a matter of what does and does not stay together at death and what simply is given up or filed and stored. The part that was animating the acted, invented persona continues; the persona itself is stored away along with its unique experiences. It survives as memories, like a wardrobe of clothes once worn and now put into mothballs.

So you can forget the idea of the current you, as you might like to think of yourself, surviving beyond death and then occupying another body because you are mostly a collection of thoughts and memories,

padded out with a persona and running on a consciousness injected from your <u>higher self,</u> to use a phrase
in common use here. I am going to explain this from
a few angles to avoid any misunderstanding because
it would be easy for some to think I am saying you
are not a spiritual being; I am not saying this at all.
I am saying that you need to get clear on what you
really are through all eternity. I am most certainly not
going to be Ian Fenn for an eternity; even he would
not wish that on himself. (This is Ian and I agree with
my higher self here; I do not wish to be this limited
for an eternity.—Author's note)

Let's look again at the past life idea. If you had past
lives, what part of them was you? (By that I mean the
<u>you</u> reading this book.) They may have had a different
sex perhaps; they certainly had a different body. They
had another personality, they had their own thoughts
and feelings, and they had a whole life of memories.
They had another mother and father and sisters and
brothers. They would have had their own little quirky
ways and special fears. They may have been Chinese,
Russian, German, or alien. They may have hated the
foods you love and been skilled in ways you are not.
They had interests in certain hobbies that you know
nothing and care nothing about. In short, each one
was not any part of you in any real human sense. The

only part that is common to all of these past-life experiences is the being that runs them, the consciousness that flows through them. So can <u>you</u> become enlightened? Have <u>you</u> had past lives? Can <u>you</u> experience immortality? This is where we need to get clear on <u>who you really are.</u>

Now when Ian Fenn (the human I used to write this book) finally grasped this, he was not upset, for he had suspected it for some time. He really found it liberating because he knew that the core being he had experienced all of his life was, in fact, the true him and that in every sense he was truly the immortal being. Until you can grasp this idea—that you, in the sense that the average person thinks of themselves as being, are not the part that survives for eternity—then you will continue to believe that chanting or yoga, for example, will lead to enlightenment. The part that could be enlightened is already there and always was and always will be; one of its bodies chanting "OM" will not make it more of a super being than it already was.

Okay, so we have looked at what you are not; let's look at what you are. You are created to complete a task in the game of the universe, like chess pieces, and your true purpose is to search for keys in the game. Not all are created equal, just like chess pieces are made with different powers. There are the king and queen and the pawns and all those in between.

I have no doubt that this will upset some and lead others to a state of smug knowingness. The thing is that the ego or, more accurately, the mind's collected images of itself combined with its need to survive lead it to feel superior often beyond its real power or capabilities.

A great example of this is that most car drivers are very average; as Ian Fenn, I can say this because I spent many years racing motorcycles. Having your knee on the ground at over a hundred miles an hour surrounded by other racers all fighting to be in front of you requires a level of skill way beyond the average car driver or motorcyclist's. However, just about every driver believes they have great driving skills and cat-like reflexes, and if you speak of poor drivers, they will agree with you that most other drivers are dreadful and they will have stories to prove it. In other words, just about every driver believes they are in the top 10 percent of skilled drivers. So what I am about to tell you will be taken by many in the same way; consider this when placing yourself in the scheme of things.

Before we make judgments on the various states of a human being that I am about to describe, I feel the need to remind you that the only real, long-term, surviving part of any person is what you refer to as **their** soul (which is, of course, putting the cart before the horse). This being the case then, if the soul energy invested in a particular human is a large amount or a small amount, it is no different in terms of what it is; it is just varying in quantity, in the same way a piece of pure gold is pure gold regardless of its weight.

The only force that allows any consciousness in a human is that which is projected into it from the bigger being who is operating it. I wanted to stress this in case the following information causes some of you to feel somehow more than any other. The true spiritual aspect of you is the same regardless of how much has been projected into you; some do have more and some less, but volume is not, in this case, a thing to be competitive about.

The reason we have these differing human states of consciousness has to do with the rules of the game, which, firstly, state that he who escapes the universe with the least lives used and in the shortest time will be the overall winner of any round of the game called "The Universe."

There are also some extra rules about the lives we can create just to make things more interesting; this takes the form of a point system.

Humans, for example, have three point-sizes for scoring, and the idea is to use the least number of points in order to collect all the keys hidden on Earth. The largest point-size for a human is a thousand and the smallest is one point. The third and final size is ten points. So how does this point system work and what is the point (pun intended)? Having given all the beings you can create on all the millions of planets in the game a point value, it then becomes clear that the lower your point score, the better you have done.

What follows is a description of the characteristics of the various humans we can make to play the game through. The body type is not a consideration and plays no part in the point-value; it is only the amount of consciousness and the depth of connection we flow into it and allow back and forth from it to us that gives it the various scores.

THE ONE POINT HUMAN

The One-Point Human

One-point humans are everywhere and are by far the most common of all humans to be created throughout history so far.

They are autonomous beings, they make their own choices, and they have a strong ego system to ensure survival. One-point humans generally follow the herd in most things they do; although they do make choices they are nonetheless choosing from the menu of life set before them. They are most likely to follow a mass religion and stay in it all of their life. They will be aligned with a political party but not actively involved. It is doubtful they will have ever studied the policies of the party in any detail and will in the main not change their political view from that of their parents. Neither will they be likely to switch from what their social circumstances would suggest for them, unless the party is in charge during a big downturn, at which time they can be persuaded to change allegiance en masse. They are typically conservative in nature and opinion, and do not want to rock the boat. They can appear intelligent by the usual definition of the word, in that they can study facts and courses and learn systems and methods, even, for example, becoming a computer-code writer or designer of complex software (as long as they are simply using code written by others, as opposed to being the inventors of a whole new way of programming), none of which truly shows creative intelligence, which is the ability to invent entirely new ways of thinking or creating a totally original thought.

A rat can learn to find its way through a complex maze with the correct training. True intelligence without spiritual consciousness does not really exist. The ability to learn and reason also belongs to insects. You can study all the course materials on quantum physics, for example, and take an exam based on what you have been given. This then allows you to say you have a degree in quantum physics. However, there are only a few people who ever invent new sciences or progress any science beyond its agreed-on frontiers, and that is the true sign of intelligence at work. My point being here that a one-point human is not a stupid human; it is more that a one-point human is not normally an explorer and does not usually discover anything new unless they simply stumble on to it. They are not usually risk-takers and entrepreneurs. Mainly, they don't do much that is outside the box.

As a player of the game, this type of human is created to use as a low-risk way of looking for the keys hidden on Earth. On other planets, there are similar native beings with similar point values. One-pointers can be used to make general searches for keys, and it is hard to describe what happens when you get close to a key other than it is simply a feeling, like when you play the game with a child of hiding something and then telling them they are getting warmer or colder as they walk around searching. You get an intuitive feeling that a certain experience is close to being a key. I have said already that keys are not some physical item; they are experiences. Not all keys on Earth are experienced by humans; at one time, you could gain a key from being a tyrannosaurus rex. Recently, however, apart from the keys held by the dolphin and whale people, the main keys are experiences had by humans.

THE TEN POINT HUMAN

The Ten-Point Human

Ten-point humans are different in that the amount of awareness being flowed into them allows for an element of steering that is not available when you run a one-pointer. The amount of consciousness you are flowing into one of these ten-pointers is tenfold, and this is where the score system gets its point values. This type of human has a connection to you in that it can access information from other beings you are running, it can sense its greater self, which is you, the immortal being running it, and because of this, it is mostly unhappy. Unlike the one-pointers, who are not connected enough to sense much of a psychic nature, the ten-pointers have just enough that they know that all is not what it seems; they are half-awake because they are physical beings but they have the spiritual consciousness flowing into them to such a degree that they know things, but they don't have any evidence to support why they know things. They are the great seekers to help you find keys because they are driven to seek the answer, to find out what it is they are sure they are missing. They are, because of this, often great adventurers and travelers.

They will often study many spiritual paths and have many career changes. They can start businesses and be full of ideas on new ways to make money. They can even start their own religions or at least their own spiritual study systems, some of which may be for money and some for the reason that they truly believe they are special and have something to give mankind. The ego mixed with this level of spiritual energy and consciousness makes for many a new guru. They can also be great leaders, taking whole nations into greater freedom or into utter destruction.

The ten-pointer is very much in evidence at this time because the Earth has a lot of attention focused upon it as certain keys have become available due to the particular moment in history, and ten-pointers are your best bet when you sense a key is at hand. Some ten-pointers even arrive here from other planets in spaceships, and some of them have come to attempt to stop others from gaining the keys that their creators already have. When so many super beings are playing in the universe, the game can get very interesting, like a giant game of chess.

Ten-pointers will spend their lives in a restless mode of operation and will never be content with what they have. They just know that being human stuck on Earth is not their natural state; they know because they are connected to their immortality and their creator, who is the being running them. The problem for them is that the communication is only partial and allows them to connect with the other creations of the being who is operating them all, but not directly with their creator. This connection with the others occurs during sleep and maybe in the occasional out-of-body or external experience, but it always leaves them haunted and wanting more. It is like being shown the pages of a book that explains all of life's mysteries one page at a time, and then promptly forgetting it. You just know there is something greater but can't quite put it all together.

It is no wonder they are the seekers, the eternal restless ones, and, as I said, it makes them great searchers of keys. Keys, as I have explained, are mostly experiences, and the ten-pointer is out to experience everything possible in their search for deeper meaning and deeper connection to the knowingness that the larger flow of consciousness brings them.

We can have much greater control over the ten-point human, so that when we get a sense that a key can be gained from the circumstances that are being created, and we get the feeling that we are getting warmer in our search, it is easier to exert influence and nudge or steer them toward the desired experience. It is possible to transform a ten-pointer into the next level of human; under certain circumstances, it may be a desirable option. It happens very rarely and, when it does, the human in question might announce he has become God-conscious or that he has transcended. This can cause more problems than it is worth and stop the location and experiencing of the key that was close at hand. This is why it is a rarely used technique. Not having been born with and gotten used to the thousand-point level of awareness, and suddenly having it enter you when you are a mature human, can be just too much for the mind and personality that has already developed.

THE THOUSAND-POINT HUMAN

A thousand-point human is used sparingly in the game simply because of the excessive amount of points they accumulate for the player. They can, however, appear en masse when a certain key cannot be gained by lesser-connected beings. There can be instances when entire planets have been full of thousand-point beings. It is very rare and so far has never happened in this particular galaxy, although there was once an inci-dence of it on a small moon with a settlement of only three thousand people. These occurrences are when an experience can only be had by a fully aware being (as aware as a being is allowed to be in the game).

Thousand-point humans are normally very creative; they tend to be inventors, highly imaginative writers, entrepreneurs, explorers, ground-breaking scientists, mathematical geniuses, musical composers who create new kinds of music, future thinkers, noted philosophers, rebels whose thoughts free people, amazing artists of all kinds, cutting-edge designers, brave warriors, global explorers, space explorers, and anyone who really, truly pushes human (or alien) endeavor to new heights. In short, those who not only think or act out-side the box, but they don't even see the box in the first

place. They are beyond all normal limits and are lov-
ing, kind, gentle, caring, nurturing, calm, happy, and
non-aggressive (unless in defense of loved ones). They
can appear opinionated but only to those of heavily
fixed opinion. They will mostly be confident but gra-
cious, certain but allowing. They never attack in the
name of justifying their own beliefs, edicts, or schools
of thought. In other words, they are fun-loving, kind
souls who boldly travel to new frontiers. This is not to
say, however, that they would appear saintly; they are
quite likely, because of their rebellious nature, to kick
and scream against rules and regulations. They may
even be drinkers and crazy party people at some stage
in life. Being quiet and well-mannered is often a sign
of a suppressed person, especially when circumstances
call for a more outrageous response.

These traits are a guide to what the various point-
humans will display, and are not meant as definite
indication; some of the traits mentioned often cross
over between ten- and one-thousand pointers, but
hardly ever between a one and a thousand.

We would use a thousand-point human when we
need our creation to be the one leading from the front,
when we want a being capable of not only experiencing
a key but often being the first one to do so. Someone

has to be the first to experience any key so that others may follow, and sometimes the only being that can experience a certain key is the one who invents it, for the experience of being the first is sometimes a key in itself.

"I awoke to find myself in this new place of swirling particles flying in all directions, impacting and growing, collecting together and then flying apart. The first thing I remember was expanding myself to fill the whole of the space and at the same time having my attention on what the tiniest speck of dancing energy was up to. As I filled the universe with my attention, I could feel something unfamiliar to me: edges!"

CHAPTER SEVEN

THE KEYS AND WHAT THEY MAY BE.

Keys in the game of the universe, as I have mentioned, are mostly experiences and very rarely are they actual objects, but you never know what they are going to be or where they are to be found because, of course, it is a mystery game, after all. I have been playing the game now for around eighteen billion years. As you may know, the universe has not always had the circumstances that would make a flesh-and-bone life form possible or even a single-cell creature. The first opportunity to experience a key, therefore, was not to be found on a planet at all.

The idea that in the beginning was darkness is not a true statement; in fact, in the beginning was a giant super-hot plasma ball, which was caused by a massive amount of normal energy being suddenly compressed. This happened when, for want of an easy description, the balloon was inflated and the dense universe was made. The immortal beings who had joined the game all came into this newly made region with their freshly wiped memories. As they awoke from a momentary induced sleep period, they began to wander around in these new conditions, where there was nothing but possibilities, a vast area of possible futures that could go in a million directions. The future was unknown and mysterious, unless you happened to be the Game Maker or one of his helpers.

In the worlds the players had left behind, all possibilities could be and often were instantly manifested. Their native universe responded to the slightest thought and there was never a need to wait for anything to be created. Now, they were not really interested in manifesting sports cars, money, power, or any other goals of a human. There is no need for things as support mechanisms, and nothing that is a solid form is needed for your continued survival in that world. When you are immortal, you have no real need of anything. You simply are, and that is that. However, if you did think up an object or a story of some kind, it would instantly be made before you. In this new place in which the players found themselves, it was not nearly so responsive, and this was disorienting and puzzling.

The players all instinctively knew that they could influence the world around them, but because they had voluntarily lost the memory of what they were normally capable of doing, they had no idea just how fast this used to happen for them.

They also had no idea why they were in this new place, but after a very short time, they all had a feeling that they must try to get out, that all was not what it should be. But where exactly was this place and what was it all about?

The game had begun, and because of the math that had been built into the basic structure of this universe, things would begin to change very quickly.

There followed a period of formation as the built-in math and laws, which could also be called pre-programmed instructions, began to do their work. The giant plasma ball that was the early universe began to cool and as it did so, the basic instructions needed to begin creating everything flowed into it in the form of frequencies; these were transmitted by the Game Maker. These special frequencies acted upon the raw energy, and where the frequencies crossed each other, they begin to form localized interference patterns.

In other words, the first basic particles of matter began to appear. To put it another way, raw energy was taking form. A universe of forms was emerging, starting with the tiniest particles, the building blocks of a place to be filled with objects that could endure through time.

I awoke to find myself in this new place of swirling particles flying in all directions, impacting and growing, collecting together and then flying apart. The first thing I remember was expanding myself to fill the whole of the space and at the same time having my attention on what the tiniest speck of dancing energy was up to. As I filled the universe with my attention, I could feel something unfamiliar to me: edges! I could sense that I was contained, restricted...and it was uncomfortable. The place was strange indeed, for it had a definite size. I felt all around the edges of what you know as your entire universe in a matter of moments, and I quickly located an area of difference. I moved my attention to this place and found what is best described as a tunnel. The entrance to the tunnel was small compared to the whole of the space, and as I moved all of my attention into it, I became aware of myself as having mass and size. I was a ball of energy now and from the outside I might have appeared to be glowing brightly. I headed up the tunnel and came to a door at the end. In fact, the door was an energy field, and I sensed a being was around the door blocking my way through.

"I wish to pass," I told the being with a thought, and a thought returned instantly: "You do not have the keys to leave this place. You are incomplete." I had no idea what this meant. Keys? Incomplete? "Who are you?" I asked. "I am the gatekeeper and you are incomplete," came the answer. "I wish to leave this place. Please move out of my way immediately." "Please return with the keys and you shall be allowed to leave," it said.

"Why am I here and what is this place?" "You are here because you asked to be here; you are here to find the way back out, and to do so you must go back and find the keys."

That was the first of many, many visits I made to the gatekeeper in the early times, just asking the same questions: why am I here and who am I? You see, the question you all have about yourselves is built into this place. At first I kept thinking it was a mistake or maybe some cosmic joke; however, there was never a different response from the gatekeeper, and there was no way to force past the door.

The first keys showed up quite soon as the experience of being an early star, burning brightly and creating effects on the energy and space around me. The first keys were simply experiencing yourself as parts, not as the whole—getting used to being a small object, even the tiniest of objects, as opposed to the entire universe all at once. When you shrank your awareness down to the size of a star, you had an instinctive knowing that this experience was a key, one of the keys you had been told to seek. That was, for me and the other players, the start of the very long search for all the keys that would be needed to get past the gatekeeper.

Though the keys are nearly always experiences, there are a few that are solid objects; there have been times when players have found one of these objects and, in a competitive spirit, decided to hide it from the other players. They do this in order to cause their competitors to use up as many lives as possible search-ing for it. One such key was hidden beneath the pyr-amids of South America—or was it the pyramids of Egypt? I forget now…well, actually, I am not allowed to say. There is a tower seven miles high built on top of one of these objects on a very distant planet, and there is also an object on the far side of your moon, where there is much evidence of past mining activ-ity. In fact, this solar system of yours has four of the thirty-three known objects in this galaxy. This is one of the reasons it is subject to so much activity, and that includes visitors from other parts of space and even other-dimensional variations of this universe (more on that later). However, the biggest single reason that this planet has a lot of attention right now is you— you humans, that is. Humans are such a rich source of keys with just the right amount of so many things: a large brain and developed senses, a tendency to love and nurture, a need for social interaction and group living, and a developed sense of self or what some call the ego, the darker side that drives ambition, and the need for power that leads to wars and all kinds of drama. The human is not unique in any of these traits, apart from the fact that they seldom all appear in one species at the same time and with such intensity.

The time is ripe now, with the development of various technologies, for experiences that cannot be had during any other period in your Earth's history.

The difference of the experience of being a plant-eating dinosaur fighting to the death to protect its young from a fierce carnivore such as T Rex and the experience of trying to get your human children to safety during an alien invasion have many similarities, but the mental nuances are quite, quite different. Both experiences have already been had here on Earth by many game players.

There are many types of keys to be experienced in the game; they are spread across the billions of galaxies and, of course, I cannot list them all. It is only required of each player to gather around fifty thousand keys in total before they can get past the gatekeeper and back to the place they previously called home and complete the game. Because the many experiences that occur on different planets, in different galaxies, and with unrecognizable species do not easily translate into this culture, it is easier for the purposes of explaining the nature of the keys to stick to speaking about Earth keys.

I have learned from previous discussions with humans that you tend to think a key experience has to be some dramatic event, but in truth they can appear to be very mundane. The key experiences can appear ordinary because you are very used to them on this planet. You might, for example, think that surviving a lifetime in a primitive culture is not that interesting. But, in fact, a place and time where wild animals are sizing you up for dinner most days can offer key experiences, especially in a complex social structure that works together with others to ensure the group's safety. This is entirely different from being a grazing animal that becomes a lion's lunch.

Other so-called mundane experiences, like coping with the ever-faster pace of life in business in these hectic, troubled times, offer other key experiences not possible in the more rural settings of three hundred years ago. Some keys can be very dramatic and require special circumstances to act them out. The key gained by putting yourself directly in harm's way, risking almost certain death to save your friends or family, having the feeling that you no longer care more about your physical form than you care for the safety of others, is quite a prized key because it is only possible in rare situations. I personally got this key on another planet and did not come to Earth to get it, but some of the players are currently making humans in order to have this very rare experience. That is why Earth at this time is so special because there have been many opportunities to gain this particular key in your recent history. The chance to experience this key has been occurring way back in human history, but the difference is that with so few people on the planet before the recent population boom, there was hardly any lifetime that would allow this experience to be had. Now that there are billions of humans, chances to be the ultimate warrior hero have increased a thousandfold.

I think you can see the key experiences are many and varied, and I am not at liberty to list them all, but know this: I made Ian Fenn, the writer of this book, to experience as many of them as possible in one lifetime, and one of the more difficult experiences to be had from the human form is risking life and limb just for the sheer fun of it.

This is very different from the warrior urge that involves risking yourself in acts of war, and also has nothing to do with lofty ideals and egocentric belief systems that one has value only in the measure to which he is willing to go to protect his nation's ideals. Or the sheer act of unselfish love in placing yourself in mortal danger to save your family. No, the key that is experienced through a no-fear attitude of risking your life just to have fun is normally expressed more in sports, like motor racing or sky diving, for example. That is why I guided Ian to become a motorcycle racer, and I can tell you it is one of the more fun keys to be collected. You can see why certain times and the technical developments they bring can have such great opportunities to collect particular keys. If you want to experience how it feels to risk death just for the fun of it, then finding a culture that not only thinks this acceptable but positively encourages it is a definite bonus, I am sure you would agree.

This key is easy to find on any racetrack at this time: sitting on the start line, engines revving, surrounded by others who are all intent on getting into that first bend at the end of the start straight before you do. Sitting on top of so much snarling, churning steel and rubber, laid on its side at a hundred miles an hour with your knee sliders scraping on the floor, knowing that if you make a mistake, you could be seriously injured or even killed is such a fabulous experience. It is an experience that cannot be had outside this universe because until you have become a being that can be hurt or even die from an activity, then how can racing a motorcycle be at all exciting? It is always the possibility of death that makes racing so much fun; it is not the winning or the glory. It is because you can die; that makes racing motorcycles or any other superfast vehicle so much fun. Anyone who tries to tell you otherwise does not have the slightest clue what it is all about.

Imagine for a moment that you cannot die, you cannot be harmed at all. Would racing a motorcycle be exciting? Imagine that you can drive as fast as you like; you can leave your braking until as late as you like when approaching a bend because if you do misjudge it and fall off, it does not matter. Imagine that no forces at all can hurt you. What would be the risk? What would be the excitement? That is exactly why beings like us are playing the game. That is why being human is so much fun.

That is why a key from this particular planet is so special: fun and joy mixed with risk and suffering.

Peace and war, laughter and tears, freedom and prison, success and failure, power and weakness, abundance and poverty, love and hate: it's all here to be experienced, and all of these experiences carry the chance of another key.

When I speak of the final goal, which is gaining all the keys and finally leaving this forgetful universe, it could be easily forgotten that the game is actually the reason for it all: the playing and enjoyment of the game is actually why it is played. If any game were just about the end result, it would be far simpler to cut to the end and throw a coin in the air: heads, you win; tails, you lose. Racing a motorcycle is not about crossing the finish line in front of the pack, although that is the aim. The real fun is in the build-up to the race, meeting your fellow players the night before, the camaraderie and the jibes with each other about who is going to whip whose ass the next day. The fun of waking up to a crisp, fresh morning and seeing that the track will be dry all day. Hearing the starting of so many highly tuned race engines before the first practice laps of the day begin. The gathering of riders in the pit lane and the pre-race butterflies in the bottom of your stomach. Then the dropping flag and experiencing the red mist of momentary insanity coming down over your eyes as the high-speed, high-octane dance of leather-clad warriors aboard ultra-powerful metal horses ensues. Lap after lap, pushing all the limits of physics to the very edge of what is possible. This is the reason we race, not to gather trophies and garlands. This is the reason we enter the game of the universe: for the sheer fun of it.

This is why I sit and write this book, not for any accolade and certainly not just to finish it— for, once it is finished, then it is done. The enjoyment of making things happen, of overcoming the difficulties is the actual experience. As Ian Fenn, I have boxes and boxes of trophies from my racing days, but I never raced for bits of metal, plastic, and marble. Keys are the same as trophies in that they are evidence of experiences, reminders of fun and the greatest of times.

The box of trophies becomes the box of keys; however, rather than a box of objects, it is the vibration, the essence of the experiences, that is stored in our surrounding energy field. This is what the gatekeeper can read when a player goes to see him at the end of the tunnel. The gatekeeper can read the vibrations and can see if the player has enough of the key experiences to leave the universe.

I miss the racing days as Ian Fenn, just as I miss the many millions of incredible days on all the other worlds. I understand why so many beings love to play the game of the universe over and over.

So I think you now have an idea of what a key might be, and maybe you believe me, or you are not sure. But ask yourself this: if life is not a search for experiences, rich incredible, wonderful experiences, then what is it about? Is it making yourself as comfortable as possible while you wait for your inevitable death? What seems more likely to you, that the whole of creation was an accident? Or perhaps you think that it was all made as a test to see if humans are good during one small, extremely short life, a single life on one small planet, in one small galaxy, and then followed by a trillion years in heaven or hell as exactly the same person you are right now (only with wings and a harp). One life, after which you will be judged by some all-powerful but judgmental and severely vindictive God-being.

Or is it what I am telling you: that, as immortal beings, we are fun-loving and invent new ways to experience a million different aspects of ourselves throughout eternity?

Are we gods playing games, laughing, and dancing together with smiles that cross not just our human faces but the dimensions of time and space forever?

"Maybe you have read every book by every guru, modern or ancient (actually, that would be impossible since most of them don't live on this planet or even abide in this galaxy), and even after having read every page a dozen times, you still feel that someone out there must have written some words that can free you even more."

CHAPTER EIGHT

WHAT IF THE GAME IS REAL?

I think some of you by now have a feeling that it is indeed real, or at least some part of it is.

I know that some of you like this explanation of the universe you live in, but there seems to be some conflicting data with other ideas you may already have about what you are and how and why you are here. I think it would help you to merge this new idea with your current reality if I can throw some more light on how it all works, especially regarding how you can be one of many limited creations and yet at the same time you are the super being. This apparent separation is a deliberate choice and a necessary function of the game. The reason is that in order to experience, for example, what the sheer fear and excitement of racing a motorcycle can feel like, there has to be the appearance of and belief in a real and serious threat to your continued existence. This requires knowingness and unknowingness at the same time.

So let us assume that you think you are an immortal being of some kind, but you don't understand why it is you are apparently trapped here, waiting for death to finally know the truth. Perhaps if you are lucky you have had a peak experience, when for a few brief hours before the doubts crept in again, you had a glimpse of your immortal self and you had no doubt that you are indeed a spiritual being. Perhaps you have had dreams that came true; perhaps you have had an angel walk up to you and tell you something you needed to hear. Maybe during meditation you felt external to the body or even had the viewpoint of being outside of the body completely, for a brief time or many times. Perhaps as a child you had experiences with invisible friends or visited other worlds as you fell asleep.

Perhaps you have had more incredible journeys or happenings, like a friend of mine experienced, when he was instantly transported from a life-threatening situation to a safe place several miles away and had no idea how he got there, no idea what saved him.

You may not have had any of the experiences I described, but you have an unshakable knowing instead that you will survive death, that you are more than just a human.

Whatever your experiences have been that led you to believe you are going to live beyond the death of your body, obviously they have resulted in your interest in books such as this one. Maybe you have read every book by every guru, modern or ancient (actually, that would be impossible since most of them don't live on this planet or even abide in this galaxy), and even after having read every page a dozen times, you still feel that someone out there must have written some words that can free you even more. You are looking for _the_ book or _the_ teacher that finally helps you to experience the missing secret to your true identity.

Maybe you have followed a ten-step, nine-step, or twenty-step path to enlightenment and reached the top or have given up after a short time, feeling let down. These multi-step teachings, in which each step is holding out the promise that this step is the one that will finally bring it all together, can often hold a person for his or her entire life.

This is the story of the seeker, or the half-god, half-flesh creation, and it is the same to one degree or another across the whole of this universe and the other vibrational worlds that surround it.

What I am saying here is that the ideas we have explored as a story are more truth than fiction, and because we sense this or even know this while trapped in the game and its deliberately limited environment, it leads to a confusion that has created many misunderstandings. You can often feel even more confused when you are the thousand-point human than when you are the one-point human for the reason that your sense and intuition is so much more developed, and yet it still does not manage to reveal the whole truth. The knowingness it brings can lead us to believe that one day humanity could become superhuman, could bend spoons or larger objects by mind power, and that we could levitate or even fly like Superman.

Let us look at a few home truths about this. Have you met a human who can fly? Have you met a human who can really levitate? And let's be clear: that means the body floating upwards off the ground, and not the hilarious bouncing about, crossed-legged, yogic flying, which is comical. Emperor's clothes, anyone?

I mean, really, have you seen anything on a day-to-day basis that suggests you are sharing this planet with immortal, all-powerful beings? Plenty of bullshit but not much in the way of real daily evidence, is there? There is so much half-truth and wishful think-ing going on that it's no wonder there is more than enough confusion for a thousand different teachings to prosper and make the authors, founders, and sell-ers of them multi-millionaires. This is not to say that incredible happenings don't take place all time, but in general these do not involve people moving heavy objects with the mind; instead, they are mostly expe-riences when a person, through the connection to the higher operating being, sees something, senses some-thing, or is guided to be in the right place at the right time.

I told you earlier that a human is a being with various amounts of conscious awareness flowed into it by beings like me, who are doing so to experience the keys of a giant, fabulous game. Let us look at the mechanics of that in order to understand exactly what the implications of this "truth" might mean to you.

You could ask the following: if I am just a flesh body with a brain gathering experiences that are flow-ing into a larger being, what part of me, if any, is the immortal super soul that lives forever? Why am I bothering if I am not even the real me?

The answer is this: the way you are designed is all part of a universe based on a lie, based on a forgotten truth. The truth is that the very essence of you, the very part of you that is immortal, is not normally unknowing or confused on the whole, or, in your case, in part. In the natural state of being, you are everywhere, in all things, all times, and all dimensions, all at once. The confusion and the resulting paradoxes of the super being split into parts is not a natural state. So this is why you are confused by this; you feel your essence, that which animates you, that which flows through you, and yet you think and feel yourselves to be separate. When you look in the mirror, you see a speck of flesh in a sea of galaxies and yet you say, "I'm looking good today." The very nature of the game of making small, microscopic, animated bodies and then flowing your essence into them with a mostly one-way flow of information is going to make for a mass of paradoxical issues that simply cannot be understood until you are finally told this truth. How can part of a picture ever give you the full view?

The you that is thinking and reading right now is not the whole being, and as such, although you are animated and aware, you cannot experience the whole truth of yourself until you are joined with your whole self. Your whole self is flowing its beingness into you, the human, looking for experiences through this human form—experiences that form keys.

The truth is: you are it, the whole self, and it is you. You are a creation of your super being self; the essence of you is immortal and you are not alone in the universe. None of your higher-self creations ever die. The bodies die for sure; however, as the super being, you have created yourself as a million separate parts. Each one of these is you in reality, but has a separate personality. You can and will meet all of your selves and you will be like a lost family coming together. When my Ian Fenn dies, he will find himself speaking with himself as the German, Native American Indian, Russian miner, space trader, and the other millions of "me's" I have created to experience the fun of being separated from my powers in order to play the game of the universe. When I leave this game and the lights go out on this particular universe, I shall be enriched by the sum of all this experience.

Imagine that each of these lifetimes as a human flows into one long experience known as my human phase. Not a string of separated lives, but a long experience of being human, like each of your days makes up your current life, in the same way all the lifetimes as a human add up to make my entire human life experience.

How many collections of multiple lifetimes have I accumulated as different life forms on other planets? My Ian Fenn is one of a million-million "me's." I can create a thousand "me's" at the same time and have a million different lifetimes on just one planet, but not always as the same type of life form.

The one thing that is common in every one of these created beings is me, the immortal being.

Is this all real to you? If not then consider that you may be more influenced by paths such as Buddhism or other main stream religions than you realize, one of which has no reincarnation and others which have some. But, really, there are no half-measures in being immortal; you either live for all eternity or you don't. If you do then the idea of one lifetime or the idea of a few makes no sense at all. The idea that you only live on one planet is also extremely limited. This is one of the main messages I am here to share and to help you expand your idea of your nature beyond Earth and beyond humanity into your eternal nature.

So let us look at the question of you in eternity, or the reality of you being an eternal being. Right now you have just one real awareness of yourself, and it is the experience of being a human. The thing I need to make clear is that whole, full-powered you is not the one experiencing itself as a human right now. You are a being that has been cut off from its full self and right now, as that less-than-full-power being, you are projecting into a human form, which is reading this page using lenses made of living cells in a tiny piece of microscopic flesh you call your body. Now, let us imagine all the thousands or millions of "you's" there have been, on hundreds or thousands of planets, and in hundreds or thousands of "other realm" places like the astral worlds, or less dense matter worlds that exist side by side with this world.

There is absolutely no denying that each and every one of them would have had to have a personality, a special way of being. I imagine you might be able to visualize yourself as having different human person-alities. Can you imagine being more insect-like on an alien world? An intelligence with a culture so utterly different that the thoughts this "you" had were dis-turbing to you as a human? Can you envision being a six-foot-tall bug that spoke with the use of pherom-ones released into the air, and a series of clicks and snaps from your mandible mouthpieces? Is this just too far from your comfort zone?

How about experiencing yourself as a star? Or what about being a planet? You see, as an eternal being, you have been around when no life forms existed, even when no universe, or at least this one, existed. If you do not consider these details, you will continue to have a very small, limited view of what you are. You are either immortal and eternal or you are not; you can-not believe that you are a spiritual being that survives without the body and then not consider what it is to exist without a body or be some type of creature other than human. Humans have been around a million or two years; you are eternal.

If you truly want to get what you are all about, you must drop the notion that you are human; that notion is what will surely trap you in an endless cycle of rebirth, or at least the continued recreation of yet more humans. The whole being, including your part of the whole, must wake up and know this. This is one of the last keys, when the whole being, including all its separate creations, comes together and awakens before leaving the game.

What would the experience be with no brain, no eyes, no ears, no body, no identity that is afforded by a form? Can you imagine being totally undefined, not having a name, a home, a need for anything at all? You just are. There is just you floating in a sea of light or a sea of dark. Can you imagine existing with not one thought? Can imagine how you would think without human words, or any words at all? Do you think it is possible to think without words? Is it possible to ask a question like "what is that?" without using any words?

Thoughts without a body may be very alien indeed. But they are, in fact, more your real state of being than the one you are currently in right now. You see, the very idea of you as a human becoming enlightened means truly becoming that which you really are, a being outside of this universe, one that does not use thoughts in any sense of the way you currently do. So I ask you this question again: can you, the human, become enlightened by meditation, or by yoga positions, or by clearing out layers or packets of stuck energies, or by learning to live in the now moment? The answer is no because the only real enlightenment is to be what you were before you came into this dense-matter universe. Until that is restored, all you are doing is rearranging the furniture on the deck of a sinking ship, or maybe a less dramatic vision would be that you are attempting to make a complete thousand-piece jigsaw image but with only one hundred of the pieces in your possession. You can rearrange them any which way in a million lifetimes; it will not help. The only true enlightenment will come, the only time you will truly say, "I am whole, I am home," is when you leave this dense-energy prison of your own making. When you have the keys to leave.

I hope these questions do not seem too repetitive; however, they are truly crucial questions to explore what it really means to be immortal. If you do not imagine what it is to be a formless, eternal being that loves to explore every viewpoint and that, right now, as a single human, you are experiencing the merest speck of what that means, then you are very likely to be reading books like this and breathing in some new torturous yoga pose for many years to come. Why not realize the truth now? You are already an eternal being.

"The one thing all these experiences have in common is that they are all still experiences within the physical universe; they are all a part of the game. If you are human or in a place surrounded with things, buildings, a landscape, etc., you are still experiencing yourself in the confines of the game."

CHAPTER NINE

THE ASTRAL PLANE AND THE CONTINUATION OF THE CURRENT PERSONALITY AFTER DEATH.

You might ask this question: if Ian Fenn, or you, are simply bodies with projected awareness, why do people report near-death experiences and such? How can we fly whilst outside the human body? How can we travel in the astral or dream body yet still have a feeling of being ourselves?

Why, when I pop out, can I pop back if I am not a singular, whole, self-contained entity?

These are good questions and the answer is simple, but first let us clarify what we mean by astral, causal, or mental planes or other levels. They are also known as heaven, hell, the fourth dimension (wrongly), the dream worlds, and a whole host of other names. Simply stated, they are other places that are similar to this world with slightly different rules, but where we still have a physical appearance and singular locality, even if it is at times with three-hundred-and-sixty-degree vision. Would that about sum up your picture of what people might consider the places we go when outside the waking human state?

I would state the question of surviving after death this way: if I am simply the projected awareness of another bigger being that is my true self (albeit a subdued version and lost in a game), how come I remain a definite personality with a sense of self when I do pop out of my body and when I travel to other realms during sleep, etc.?

The answer is that the awareness is still projected, and it is your essence. Imagine a hand full of finger puppets, all made to look different, that are, in essence, the physical selves, and the fingers moving each one are all part of the same hand. In other words, you are connected to the main you, but your personal energy field and collection of memories, thought patterns, learned behaviours, and conditioned responses are held in various fields of differing wavelengths surrounding your physical form. All of your thoughts, for example, are created and reside in the mental body, or, more accurately, that part of the field that surrounds you that is the mind. There are various frequency worlds alongside this one, and you have a template of your current form and the awareness flowed into you existing simultaneously in them all. So you have being and existence as a form on several levels. These are not separate beings at all; instead, you are rather like those wooden Russian dolls. However, the same high self created all these components of you at the moment your human form began. They are like harmonics of the same musical notes. So, providing all of them are not destroyed, then the astral or dream body of Ian Fenn or you will and can continue after the death of the flesh body.

There are some experiences that can lead to confusion about these other aspects of ourselves, one of which is apparent during lucid dreams where we can often experience being another person who has no idea of our waking lives. If you practice dream studies and learn lucid dreaming, this is quite common. As Ian

Fenn, I have experienced many times when I wake up in a dream and spend hours in some other life, often not on this planet or plane, and never once during these very lucid experiences do I remember being Ian Fenn, not even for the slightest second. Upon awakening with full recall, it can be rather disconcerting. How can I be involved in such detail in another life and, while in it, not have the slightest concern about or knowledge of my life here as the waking me? What is going on in this case? The answer is that this is a crossover in awareness; it is like the finger puppet hand suddenly changing the finger that is in a particular puppet, or perhaps the sensory data is shared between fingers. It is a crossover of awareness. Does the one person (the other you) being sensed by you as a visitor have any idea it has an intruder inside it, looking through its eyes? I don't think so. I wonder, as Ian Fenn, how many times my other "me's" might be dreaming of my life. How often do they sleep only to find themselves seeing a life in Los Angeles and wondering what that was all about?

You see, it is possible to be you and be maintained beyond this body if only for the reason that you have these other vibrational bodies as well, and most are more permanent relative to the flesh form.

The one thing all these experiences have in common is that they are all still experiences within the physical universe; they are all a part of the game. If you are human or in a place surrounded with things, buildings, a landscape, etc., you are still experiencing yourself in the confines of the game. Of course, this is not going to be other than this whilst you are in a physical body of any description. If you think you are ascended and not in the game, and you are aware of having a viewpoint of a localized nature, then you are still in the game; you are not your whole self.

You may wonder what will happen to you, the reader of this book, when the higher you leaves the universe, but there is no need to be concerned. Leaving this universe will not result in the deaths of the millions of "you's" that you have been. Instead, the being of each one continues to exist. But how can this be?

This is where being fixed in a time-space universe makes this hard to understand. If we tried to explain how a television or a laptop computer worked, or even what it was for, to a primitive tribe from the Amazon jungle which was encountering modern civilization for the first time, it would still be simpler than trying to explain other-dimensional reality to a mind and consciousness currently operating in a three-dimensional, linear-time universe. So the following will not be perfect but should at least help you get a feel for what happens to all the past and present lives you led and are currently leading.

Past life recall is one of the confusing ideas that humans have in their collective thoughts and is a popular myth right now; it is a totally misunderstood phenomenon. I already mentioned the idea of having a dream where you are some other person, and during that experience there is no memory of being the current you, the one who is doing the dreaming. This is a clue to what is happening during past life recall. We are, in fact, tapping into another of your higher self's creations and instead of understanding this, because you humans do not know of your higher self creating the many selves, you tend to think of this as a past life. You believe what happens in the process is that you, as a soul, have hopped from one body to the next. This would suggest that the other "you's" no longer exist and that they are simply forgotten memories that you have somehow remembered for a moment. This occurrence is known as a past life recall or past life experience.

That would mean the person you were no longer exists, would it not? If you believe this, oh boy, are you in for a surprise when past "you's" come to meet you at the death of your flesh body; then you will see how very much alive they still are and that they are very separate and independent from you. They do not require you to exist. They do, however, owe their continued existence to your common creator, the higher you, just as your current life memories require you to keep them alive. The truth is nothing is ever lost and none of us will ever vanish; the essence of you as the child survives into adulthood as your memories, and the many "me's" and "you's" will be part of the bigger, immortal being that each of us is. We really do not die or eventually face oblivion as we become integrated into the whole of our much vaster and multidimensional selves.

AN IMPORTANT ANNOUNCE-
MENT FOLLOWS, PLEASE PAY
CLOSE ATTENTION.

Notice of Contract to Terminate Your Participation in This Universe.

We hope that this book has served the true purpose it was intended to fulfill. If it has then by now you will have the feeling that there is more truth here than fiction. You may be experiencing something like extreme déjà vu; if so, do not worry: it is simply the rhythm, energy and sequence of ideas that were put together in order to implant a wake-up call.

When you entered the game of the universe, for reasons that will become known to you, you opted for the early call or alarm call. This was intended to help (through a series of nudges and prompts) to bring you out of the hypnotic, forgetful state you have been in during the last fifteen billion years. You have been playing the game of being a defined being or beings. You are hereby put on notice that this is the **third** of these attempts to begin the waking process.

At the death of this being and the others you may be running, either here on Earth or on other planets or planes of existence allied to this universe, we invite you to go directly to the gatekeeper at the end of the tunnel. You will have no problem getting there; you will simply have to intend to be there and you and your many three-dimensional selves will be there.

When challenged by the gatekeeper that you do not have all the keys required, please inform him that the Game Maker has left your name on a list and ask him to check the early opt-out list.

You will then be able to leave the universe and travel through an energy field, where your full memory will be restored.

Please note this is the third of five messages we are obligated to insert into your game experience. If after receiving all five, you fail to make your way to the gatekeeper, we will not be held responsible for your continued entrapment. If you fail to leave, you may be required to remain here until the game ends in its intended way, which will be when you have all the keys.

Wake up—you are immortal. Wake up—it is time to leave.

Thank you on behalf of the Game Maker and his staff. We hope you have enjoyed playing with us and that you will be back to play more games very soon.

Other recommended games from the Game Maker include:

Solitaire: experience being the only being in a gigantic void for a trillion years, and then creating a universe made only of you. Experience a gazillion viewpoints, all of them yours.

Color and Music World: this one is great to play after the rigors of a physical universe. Relax for a few billion years surrounded by vast seas of flowing colors and listen to music more beautiful and varied than you ever dreamed possible. Experience yourself as a viewpoint cradled in love and bliss with nothing to do or be—in a shared world or all on your own.